W9-AOQ-394

Comparisons

To Pastor Cheryl C
Thanks for being my
friend & supporter
of my ministry too~

Conzette R Garrett
6/15/19

Comparisons

Poems that Reflect the Earthly and the Divine

COZETTE R. GARRETT

RESOURCE *Publications* · Eugene, Oregon

COMPARISONS
Poems that Reflect the Earthly and the Divine

Copyright © 2019 Cozette R. Garrett. All rights reserved. Except for brief quotations in critical publications or reviews, no part of this book may be reproduced in any manner without prior written permission from the publisher. Write: Permissions, Wipf and Stock Publishers, 199 W. 8th Ave., Suite 3, Eugene, OR 97401.

Resource Publications
An Imprint of Wipf and Stock Publishers
199 W. 8th Ave., Suite 3
Eugene, OR 97401

www.wipfandstock.com

PAPERBACK ISBN: 978-1-5326-7376-4
HARDCOVER ISBN: 978-1-5326-7377-1
EBOOK ISBN: 978-1-5326-7378-8

Manufactured in the U.S.A.   FEBRUARY 27, 2019

Scripture quotations marked NLT are taken from the Holy Bible, New Living Translation, copyright © 1996, 2004. Used by permission of Tyndale of Tyndale House Publishers, Inc.,Wheaton, Illinois 60189. All rights reserved.

Scripture quotation marked NRSV are from New Revised Standard Version Bible, copyright © 1989 National Council of the Churches of Christ in the United States of America. Used by permission. All right reserved worldwide.

Scripture quotations are from The Holy Bible, English Standard Version®, copyright © 2001 by Crossway Bibles, a publishing ministry of Good News Publishers. Used by permission. All rights reserved.

Scripture quotations marked NCV are taken from The Holy Bible, New Century Version, copyright © 2005 by Thomas Nelson, Used by permission. All rights reserved.

Scripture quotations marked NIV are taken from the Holy Bible, NEW INTERNATIONAL VERSION*. Copyright © 2011 by Biblica Inc. All rights reserved.

Scripture quotations marked AMP are taken from THE AMPLIFIED BIBLE, Copyright © 1954, 1958, 1062, 1964, 1965, 1987, by Lockman Foundation. All rights reserved. Used by permission. (www.Lockman.org)

Scripture quotations marked KJV are taken from the King James Version of the Bible.

This book is dedicated to my early life mentors:

Mrs. Birda Perkins—ex-slave, prophet, and storyteller

*Mrs Jennie Sims Broadnax Vance—music teacher, poet, sage,
and clergy spouse*

*Sister Mary Lurana, SBS—poet, artist, teacher, counselor.
and nature lover*

Contents

Words of Thanks

THANKS TO EVERY FAMILY member and friend who helped me to live life and go through hard and good times. Thanks to life coaches and teachers who showed me better ways of being and doing. Unending gratitude goes to my late parents, Willie R. and Irma Beard Rogers, and other mentors who dropped seeds of wisdom that are folded into these poems and sayings.

Thanks to the Tennessee Department of Human Services, Youth Services (now Bridges), Regional One Health Medical Center, Church Health of Memphis, Sisters of the Blessed Sacrament, First Baptist Church-Brownsville, TN, Mississippi Boulevard Christian Church (Disciples of Christ), Community of Faith Christian Church (DOC), Grace United Methodist Church, Memphis Theological Seminary, United Theological Seminary at Dayton, and Delta Sigma Theta Sorority, Inc. where I served two past terms as our Southern Regional Chaplain.

Poems came from my own reflections after *working with, learning from, and listening to* the personal stories of co-workers, friends, church members, patients/clients, sorority sisters, and faculty/students of the institutions, groups, churches, faith-based church ministries, and organizations listed above. Through attentive listening to others, I also listened more closely to my own story and often wove intimate pieces into some of these poems!

Praise to God for allowing me to serve others in varied ministry contexts as a lay person and later as clergy who heard countless stories that demonstrated suffering endured, pains overcome, and joys experienced. Thanks to the divinely inspired writers and recorders of biblical scriptures which enlightened and *continue to enlighten and transform* the paths of myself and others. Thanks to the Holy Spirit God who gave me this poetry. Glory to God!

COZETTE R. GARRETT
May 23, 2018

Introduction

FOR THE LAST THREE decades, I have listened while people have trusted me by telling me their personal, private stories. I was a social worker who processed applications for public assistance, food stamps, nursing home care, and Medicaid. I was and still am ordained clergy who listened to and am still listening to the stories of the upper middle class and the educated. I was a hospital and hospice chaplain who ministered to the mothers and fathers of newborn babies and the families of those saying goodbye to 90-year-old patients who had lived full and often complicated lives. And I have served as mentor to many and counselor/teacher to adults who were preparing for marriage, new occupations, parenthood, healthier lifestyles, life transitions (including death), financial crises, relational changes, and a balanced life in licensed/ordained ministry . . . My ministry context has been broad. Without revealing names, places or dates, all the stories from the above sources *and more* are blended into the poems in this book that tell of *human challenges, celebrations, and sometimes divinely granted new beginnings.*

Over the years, I noticed that the journeys of storytellers sometimes reflected my story! To my amazement, *the person sitting before me unknowingly told me parts of my own story as they recounted theirs*! I believed then and continue to believe that God was sending me divine hints indicating that the pains and joys of people are similar, universal, and part of the human condition.

While some stories were similar to mine, there were also those people who confidentially told me life stories that were far more challenging and complex than my own. Both in sacred and secular settings, there were narratives that were initially weighted down heavily with abuses, mistreatment, sickness . . . and unresolved issues. In some cases, after time had passed and several interventions had taken place, I could see and hear in their present stories obvious physical, emotional, relational, personal, and spiritual change. Sometimes after months or years of intervention and transformation, clients or parishioners could tell stories of surviving and thriving even in the midst of present pain or recent recovery! For some, I saw new coping skills and empowerment in families. Survivors, at any stage, inspired me by their hope and healing processes so that I have become a more positive liberated person and a stronger advocate for others.

I love to laugh! In many cases, humor and smiles prevail. I believe that readers will find themselves folded in the poems and then receive comfort in knowing that they are not alone in the universe. I hope that readers will be inspired and encouraged to discover new resources and fresh paths. Sometimes it just helps to find humor in tough situations and to laugh at one's self as we believe that things are really going to get better.

In addition to the ministry contexts mentioned above, I also served as an adjunct seminary professor, a program director in faith-based ministries, senior and associate pastor, and a wife and mother. As I continued to serve, reflect, pray, grow, and listen, I was struck by the patterns of stories. Sometimes story retelling reminded me of everyday *people, places and things. Somehow comparing the stories to objects or bible stories brought illumination or greater meaning to the messes!* As I wrote poems about the stories to which I had been listening, I first heard *hope* and later *peace* sprang from the often hell-like conditions. Sometimes, I made some sense of the harsh realities and other times, there was no peace to be found. Periodically, the Spirit reminded me that *people have free will and are permitted to make both great and poor choices.* For example, as I reflected on a number of couples with whom I counseled, I was reminded of little mice scampering to live! So, with a smile and a sigh, I wrote one of my favorites called, "Mr. and Ms. Mouse"! Somehow, I got a measure of acceptance and peace in my spirit as I meditated in the presence of the true God of Reconciliation.

Often there is or was an individual who had a great impact in my life and his or her life story became pivotal in my spiritual formation. Poems such as "The Seashell, Helen" or "To Alvin O. Jackson, the Pastor of Our Pasture" are dedicated and written as offerings to a particular person who had meaningful input in my life's development. I say thank you especially to the people to whom those poems are dedicated.

Of course, there are poems about relationships—those that tell of craziness and sorrow and also those that celebrate love, strength, and tenderness. There are poems about successful and failed friendships that resulted in feelings of great loneliness or sweet sanctuary.

My book, *Comparisons,* has poems that are divided into two sections. *Part I* is named "Earthly Commonplace Challenges"

Part II is called "Divine Renewals and Celebrations"

In order to remain positive, optimistic, and balanced, I suggest that you alternate reading from Parts I and II. At one sitting, perhaps you might want to read at least one poem from each section as you reflect on the meaning of each poem. Remember, God has challenges *and* celebrations cradled in God's hands!

I believe that the Holy Spirit blew on decades of conversations and on my listening so that I began to notice patterns and commonalities in the problems and solutions that people discovered. Certainly, situations are viewed through a woman's eyes but poems reflect the stories of the many men *and* women with whom I did and do ministry. In this collection of poems, I recall the essence of the stories and give them back to all of us so that we may examine and feel the power and presence of God. Our Savior helped people in the past and *will help us all in the future* to overcome challenges and to live into newness of life.

I have concluded that Our Divine Friend is listening to all of us and wants to bring us to places of greater acceptance and peace in the midst of our multiple storms *and* multi-faceted celebrations. Even though the words of my poems are Christian in focus, I believe that all people of faith will resonate with the truth that is in them.

I also believe that God inspired these poetic offerings because some of them were written in a few minutes and there was no need for rewrites or much labor. Other poems took months or 30 years for them to come to completion and even at this writing I am struggling to stop revising or refreshing them! I suppose I will be re-writing some of them until my death. Regardless of the time that it took to hear and write them, all poems or even the one-line sayings were and are songs from My Sacred Heart and the Holy Spirit of the bible. I have indicated when I think that there are related biblical references which might bring greater understanding or enlightenment to readers. You are encouraged to explore, meditate, and grow while reading *Comparisons: Poems that Reflect the Earthly and the Divine*.

PART I

Earthly Commonplace Challenges

How frail is humanity!
How short is life, how full of trouble!
We blossom like a flower and then whither.
Like a passing shadow, we quickly disappear.
JOB 14: 1–2 NLT

The Pink Welcome Doormat

On me your print was left.
On me your dirt was swept.

On me your fatted babies were pounded.
On me your botched dreams were mounded.

On me your rain was splashed.
On me your pests were smashed.

On me your valued guests were weighted.
On me your lewd whore was baited.

On me your ice was caked.
On me your leaves were raked.

On me your hail pelted.
On me your snow melted.

*

Mr. and Ms. Mouse

Frenzy, frazzle, fuss, bother
Pressured, pulled, and pushed;

Fluster, fumble, fret, smother
Mashed, maimed, and squished***

Falter, frailty, fray, flutter
Starved, stalked, and stretched;

Flurry, fodder, flip, putter
Blind, bold, and pressed***

Greed, fidget, fright, scamper
Tested, trapped, and teased;

Breed, furor, flinch, gather
Wetted, shocked, and squeezed***

Gnaw, flicker, flee, batter
Crazed, cramped, and crouched;

Fluff, flirter, flit, batter
Scuffled, chased, and pounced.

*

WHILE SERVING AS A chaplain and an associate pastor, a number of couples came to me for marital counseling. As I listened to stories and reports of tensions, the people reminded me of tiny mice trying to find their ways while avoiding traps and dodging cats!

To the Tongue

A lane
    lathe
    laser,
A lamprey
    larva
    lance,
A leech
    Legion
    lesion,
A ledge
    leaven
    leopard,
A lye
    limelight
    lion,
A lynx
    lizard
    litter,

A locust

   Loki

   load,

A logbook

   lobster

   louse

A loon

   lucre

   Lupus,

A lump

   lugworm

   lumpfish,

A lifetime

   lynching

   lingering,

A laud

   lust

   launch,

A lick

   lift

   lip,

A lace

   lei

   laver,

A lantern

   laurel

   lark,

A leash

   leisure

   leaflet,

A lens

   lever

   leather,

A lime

   limestone

   lyrebird,

A lilt

   lily

linden,

A lotus

lof

loaf,

A locket

loincloth

lightbulb,

A luau

lumen

loom,

A lung

lifeboat

lovebird.

"Death and life are in the power of the tongue . . ."
PROVERBS 18: 21A KJV

The Simple Warrior

Eat a scrap or two from somebody's table;

Sleep a night or two in some poor stable;

Mend a heart or two as you are able;

Save a child or two with a wise-word cable.

*

For the poor in body and spirit, except for the freely given Bread of Life, there are

no truly non-perishable food items . . .

*

Sudden Belly-Up Pressures

When bankruptcy occurs

     and you lose all your stuff

     it's always abrupt

No matter how long it took to culminate

          and

          happen.

When divorce results

     and your soul cries, "Enough!"

     it's always abrupt

No matter how long it took to culminate

          and

          happen.

When natural disaster erupts

     and your surroundings disrupt

     it's always abrupt

No matter how long it took to culminate

         and

         happen.

When Hospice shows up

     and your health dries up

     it's always abrupt

No matter how long it took to culminate

         and

         happen.

When death occurs

     and your loved one leaves us

     it's always abrupt

No matter how long it took to culminate

         and

         happen.

When relationships rupture

    and your connection interrupts

    it's always abrupt

No matter how long it took to culminate

        and

        happen.

When dreams burst

    and your plans crush

    it's always abrupt

No matter how long it took to culminate

        and

        happen.

When the enemy occupies and pushes through

    God remains, renews, untangles you . . .

No matter how long it takes to culminate

        and

        happen.

Then you will walk on your way securely and your foot will not stumble. If you sit down, you will not be afraid; when you lie down, your sleep will be sweet. Do not be afraid of sudden panic, or of the storm that strikes the wicked; for the Lord will be your confidence and will keep your foot from being caught.

PROV 3: 23–25 NRSV

The Abusive Mosquito—

Bites

> Not enough to maim, kill, or destroy

> but

> Just enough to sting, itch, and annoy;

Stays

> Long enough to use, suck, and confuse

> but

> Brief enough to limit, scar, and misuse;

Leaves

> Quick enough to hide, plant doubt, and swell fears

> but

> Quiet enough to sneak, appear harmless, and bring tears.

Steals joy, injects venom, leaves welts . . . and disappears into the night!

> So is the abuser.

> *

> The voices of Evil echo piercing lies.

> The mouth of God speaks Eternal Loving Truth.

> *

A Mid-Life Phase . . .

a haze,

a phrase in lays,

a craze of ways. . .

a gaze,

a glaze of grays,

a blaze of rays. . .

a maze,

a bout of bays,

a daze for days. . .

a horse's neighs—

a malaise. . .   .

[

A once-wayward, now-returning spouse is like a toddling child capturing
the quarter-inch buttons of a corduroy coat with oiled fingers.

]

A new body is an improved temple that houses a fresh soul experience.

*

Honor sometimes only comes at death. As the mental anguish was hidden from people, so the honor, so late in coming is too often hidden from the pain-bearing one.

*

A new career is a time

of changes in the middle of fears

and possible failure,

when finances and emotions are frayed...

but

opportunity knocks and locks in fresh success.

*

THESE POETIC OFFERINGS ARE companion pieces that tell of a time of great change and transition in the lives of me, my family, and in the lives of good friends. Some of these times of metamorphosis ended in divorce, death, new careers/business ventures, a pet purchase, relocations, elective surgical procedures, improved self-care and awareness, broken and healed relationships, new faith paths . . .

Woman's Impossible

Unfelt needs, broken beads, chips in nails;

Unfed sons, unpaid duns, shoe soles with holes;

Unkind mates, broken dates, tumors in wombs;

Unmade beds, uncombed heads, sweaters with snags . . .

The Rescuer urgently whispers,

"Living in my mind and soul will form a net of peace about your soul."

[]

Pain turned inward brings depression.

Pain turned outward fosters aggression.

Pain turned Upward yields understanding, power, and peace.

[]

Time brings changes that acceptance makes much easier.

You will keep in perfect peace all who trust in you, all whose thoughts are fixed on you!
Isa 26:3 NLT

The Roach

Just takin' up valu'ble space
        and breathin' precious air
Just stealin' from worthy folk
        and goin' really nowhere . . .
Oh, why do you this day live?

Just movin' fast toward nothin'
        and climbin' on the stair
Just putting' on a front
        and blowin' out hot air . . .
Oh, why use up all my time?

Just chompin' bread and grain
        and glidin' on the floor
Just gettin' close to givin'
        and grabbin' somethin' more . . .
Oh, why snatch from your own babes?

Just makin' moves for nothin'
        and divin' in your den
Just feelin' for my hind
        and lustin' for my kin . . .
Oh, how can you be my love?

Just showin' up on time
                and scaring off a rival
Just crawlin' in your crack
                and slightin' debts li'ble . . .
Oh, how can you show your face?

Just brushin' pass most guests
                and tellin' secrets kept
Just draggin' in more grit
                and dumpin' on floors swept . . .
Oh, why come here through my door?

Just movin' in more pests
                and mountin' up expense
Just bringin' shame of siblin's
                and closing up our vents . . .
Oh, how could you live with me?

Just dodgin' light and clean
                and breedin' best in rot
Just groomin' your slick self
                and showin' all you got . . .
Oh, why waste in my clean bed?

Just mappin' out my life
                and losin' your own way
Just spreadin' germs of doubt
                and preaching friends away . . .
Oh, why creep up from the floor?

Just movin' on my heart
　　　　and blowin' out my hate
Just grabbin' some more lust
　　　　and using talk for bait . . .
Oh, why shame me with your lies?

Just livin' in a shadow
　　　　and seeking more to roam
Just callin' me a whore
　　　　and leaving me at home . . .
Oh, where can I run to hide?

Just slappin' round my dreams
　　　　and sappin' my sweet fate
Just crammin' welts of joy
　　　　inside my conquered face . . .
Oh, why do I now feel love?

Just wantin' for a house
　　　　and settlin' for a trough
Just wearing rags for clothes
　　　　and cursin' those she bought . . .
Oh, Savior bust me out.

Just limpin' to the preacher
　　　　with tales of woe and shame
Just doin' it to grasp
　　　　for sanity and sane . . .
Oh, mercy this day please.

Just livin' for the day

        when poison will be sprayed

To loose me from the hurt

        that fills each awful day . . .

Oh God, save me from the deed.

AFTER WORKING FOR OVER 13 years as a counselor and trainer for social workers of the Tennessee Department of Human Services, I had heard one too many stories about the abuses, family violence, and personal pains of some of those who were sustained by public assistance. As a church minister, I continued to hear similar stories—especially those of women from all walks of life—who did not seem to be able to leave unkind, unproductive relationships like the one described above. Certainly, systemic brokenness of our society, evil generational practices, and unhealthy self-regard contribute to individual and community suffering. We all can share in a part of the blame for allowing the truth of "The Roach".

Unforgiveness

Unforgiveness is disallowing God's
hand to move
hatred and sadness

Unforgiveness is willfully stopping the Sacred Heart of Jesus
to allow blood flow and living water cleansing in dark and dingy places of
corruption

Unforgiveness is saying with insistence
that the Holy Spirit
has not the right and reason to clear a path for
New growth

Unforgiveness is denial of the cleaning work of cross
and cradled manger of Bethlehem

Unforgiveness is the obstruction of
not only justice but
the dismissal of
just sentencing in memory of Jesus'
Sacrificial Lamb's story
and glorious reign

Unforgiveness is fractured and chipped solidarity and wholeness

Unforgiveness is stoic, stagnant, unstable and
makes us
unable to grow
tall and full
rich and radiant

Unforgiveness is imprisonment in
chains of denial of
the power and peculiar perfection-ing of
God's hand on the repentant heart

Unforgiveness is the negating
of God's Authority and Sovereignty
when it comes to dismissal of charges and crimes

God forgives at God's discretion
any transgressions
but
people are unauthorized
to hold on when
God the Forgiver and Giver
has let go and granted
Divine Pardon.

We are to walk in God's will and way

No matter the consequences of offenses

God grants and gives pardon to

all of us in God's Divine Mind.

Amen So be it! So it is!

*

To My Floating Friend,
the Water Lily

I couldn't come with you but ...

If you lodged on a peninsula
I'd want you to float a bobbing bottle
over to my plot of the isthmus
Every now and then.

If you resided in a cavern
I'd want you to send an echoing yell
up to my edge of the hollow
Every once in a while.

If you lived on a star
I'd want you to sling a chipping meteor
across to my niche of the abyss
At some point.

If you grew in a pine
I'd want you to drop a decaying cone
down to my tuft of the earth
In due season.

If you settled on a pond
I'd want you to toss a splitting pad
below to my plop of the mud
Upon occasion.

*

Sibling Rivalry is—

Love that won't end

        except on the road to selling heir property

Handshakes that are firm

        except on the paths to keeping promises

Hugs that are all-encompassing

        except when politics and religion are discussed;

Total agreement about God Almighty

        but different remembrances about the same past events

Sweet tears about shared loved ones

        but bitter memories from different perspectives

Joined laughter about old jokes

        but few congruencies about childhood punchlines;

Everlasting hope for harmonious reconciliation

        but loving and detachment prevail

                in the

            prisons of disjointed pursuit

                    and

            sharp dissonant chords . . .

Alone

To be lonely is to
feel isolated in
a pool of navy blue, purple, charcoal, and indigo;

To be lonely is to be
locked in a cellblock
for weeks and months;

To be lonely is to
have no partner
with whom to
share your dreams, ideas, or intimate thoughts;

To be lonely is to be
chained in the clutches of a drug, thing,
person, place, or substance that only brings
false hope, lies, and no real laughter;

To be lonely is to be
separated and jerked
away from light, touch, and sound;

To be lonely is to

sense no Lord God,

Divine Lover,

or

Emmanuel;

To be lonely is to

float on a

lake for too long

without love expressed or hugs experienced;

To be lonely is to

sit in a large office of packed cubicles

with no doors and

no communication except

the Internet and electronic devices . . . period.

*

When Aging Happens . . .

All skin slides

   Enjoy the ride

Buy uplifts.

The body parts expand and shrink

   Stand tall . . . stretch

Take yoga.

The face wrinkles and drops

   Do not stop

Get retinol and collagen.

The hair thins, falls, greys, or grows in the wrong places

   Control it

Get assistance . . . now!

Teeth fall, gums rot, and stop working

   Resist it

Floss, get mints, and see dentists.

The legs thin, sway, and wobble

Do not hobble or fall

Take vitamins, use props, and eat spinach.

Muscles flex, knees ache, and bones break

Stretch, massage, and splint them

Oil, lubricate, trim weight, change shoes, move, and do therapy.

The stomach swells and rebels

Settle it

Eat fruit, drink water, seltzer, and nutrients.

The nose, eyes, and ears change

Admit it

Use eyeglasses, aids, drops, and sprays.

The mind slows and wanders

Reign it in

Do meditation . . . work puzzles, write, walk, caress a lover, and color.

The job-profession ends and a new part-time position begins

Meet new friends, jealous enemies, and an updated bio

Ask and receive forgiveness . . . let it go

Live, mentor, laugh, reflect, travel, grow . . .

The money dwindles and the barrel empties

But the supply does not end

Spend and give . . . less and more—wisely

but flow forward in God

until you walk out the door.

Friends die.

Cry, grieve, talk, remember, sing, and pray

Fresh hope and people

are waiting along the way

to be adopted and loved in this new day.

When aging happens

Recall

God is in the midst of the transitions

God is in a baby's eyes and smiles

God is Ancient Warrior, Mother Eagle, and New Lamb—

So it is . . .

Ode to Linnie Ada Thomas' Trip

They divide up all of your pieces
            and you leave for another land;
They put off your dreams
            and you leave for another land;
They cut up all of your plottings
                and you leave for another
    land . . . .

All that is left is a memory of a smile
                and you leave for another land;
All that is left is a wise-word spoken
                and you leave for another land;
All that is left is a wish for some changing
                and you leave for another
    land . . . .

So much to live for but yet you died . . . .
So much to plan for but still you died . . . . . .
So much to plead for but instead you died . . .
So much we prayed for but you still died . . . .
They wanted to bring gifts but business prevailed . . .
Crowds and Christ filled the room with flowers and bells . . .

And you left for another land . . . .

Amiss

A misplaced comrade is comparable to:

    missing pieces of a puzzle

    missing parts of a car

    malfunctioning pushbuttons of a computer

    malfunctioning pistons of a cylinder

    missing pillows of a couch

    missing dots of a clock

    mismatching quilt pieces of a coverlet

    mismatching pieces of cutlery

    plummeting meteor of the cosmos.

I WROTE THIS POEM in memory of a serious disagreement that I once had with a dear friend. After being estranged for a few years, I was grateful that we reconciled. However, before we did, in grief, I wrote this poem. Her initials happen to be M. P. C!

The Paradoxical Preacher

A bee

a fly,

       A sea

       a pond,

              A plume

              a stone.

An iceberg

A snowflake,

       A Great Dane

       a polecat,

              A moonbeam

              a fogbank.

A sunflower

a reed,

       A potato

       a leaf,

              A persimmon

              a grape.

A hare tail

a flint,

        An ant hill

        a mound,

                An Oak Tree

                a twig.

*

The Female Preacher's
Transformation for Service

An egg must be cracked,

broken,

emptied, and bruised

before she can be used to

carry the truth of God's Word . . .

And the scrambling, boiling, and baking

of her self-esteem,

giftedness, and confidence

must be blended, basted, and brushed

with the oil and sweet butter of the
Holy Spirit's

comfort, counsel, compassion, and
forgiveness . . .

And the chipped

and

shattered

shell pieces must be completely discarded and removed

before the rich orange yolk and the smooth solid white

can be

seasoned and served by God's Messenger

and then

tasted, swallowed, enjoyed, and consumed by hungry
people of the world.

*

O taste and see that the Lord is good!

Ps 34: 8A ESV

WASPS and Like-Kinds

Unresolved anger is like a wasp stinger

       not removed,

   a sudden piercing pain that attacks without provocation;

Unforgiveness is a lingering long-term muffled sting

          remembered,

   a swollen welt that aches with venom;

Unresolved anger, unforgiveness, and non-communication

     build and breed

        nests of intolerance and violence that are
wrapped in fear and hate—

Intolerance is an allergic reaction that flirts with deaths of the paralyzed
prey and predator

          victimized,

   a small flying terrorist that nurtures its young with spiders and
future butterflies.

*

TWENTY-FIRST CENTURY SOCIETY HAS become swollen with small-minded
people who are feeding our children, youth, and young adults a diet of
words and ideas that promote hatred, prejudice, violence, and isolation.

37

Concepts such as a world singing in "perfect harmony" and "love sweet love" seem to be outdated. This reminds the author of the little insect that can sometimes cause great fear, pain, suffering, and repulsion—even with a single bite!

The Steady Promise

Obama . . . the massive Maui Banyan Tree

Bo and Sunny . . . laughter in the midst of storms

A Grandparent Robinson-Root . . . placed to preserve history and protect posterity

Michelle . . . the tall Chicago Jackson Park's Japanese Cherry Blossom

America afterward . . . a Weeping Willow in a tumultuous snow storm

Sasha, Malia, and peers . . . sprouts of hope . . .

*

The beauty of the treetop is its height in the joy of the Dayspring.

*

May the God of hope fill you with all joy and peace as you trust in him, so that you may overflow with hope by the power of the Holy Spirit.

Romans 15:13 NIV

America in Winter

Children in cages

    Politicians and Media in rages

        but no possibilities of changes

            except God—

    Mothers and fathers incarcerated

or detained before thunderous applause of the murderous bases

        of the uncaring Coliseum crowds

    Food and hugs withheld by social workers not allowed to hold

And psychiatrists and doctors prevented from touching and telling

    of the yelling

        from babies burdened with abandonment fears and tears

So long to tenderness of the Liberated Statue whose arm is

    no longer lifted or lighted for the sake of unity or freedom

Children in cages

    Politicians and Media in rages

    but no relief in sight except as God brings reform and refocus . . .

        release—

Come Holy Spirit of the living God

Ring the liberty bell NOW

Warm the Wall of Winter Ice

Bring empowered saints to pull the cord so the spring flowers and showers
come now

       . . . and babies are finally rocked, reunited, and blanketed.

*

". . . for God gave us a spirit not of fear
but of power and love and self-control."

2 TIM 1: 7 ESV

PART II

Divine Renewals
and Celebrations

We can know that we are alive and well and facing the new day

if we will laugh at the clock

and embrace the moment

and entrust the seconds to Our God.

I Am Truth

Trust Me to do this—

    to you

    through you

        in you

        in spite of you

            with you

            within you

                for you

                forgiving you—

                in love, power, and

                        understanding.

For God has not given us a spirit of fear and timidity, but power, love and self-discipline.

2 Tim 1: 7 NLT

Life

WHAT IS LIFE but a spinning spindle of
spectacular splendor spurred on by a
Superior Being in a rush of splendid light
and twirling twists and tenacious turns?

And WHAT IS DEATH but a dip into the depth
of the dazing shelter of a dandelion
grove to delve into the midst of nothing?

But WHAT IS THE BELIEVER'S DAY except a
dazzling dab of Divine endless time that does
come after the deathly change has taken place?

Recycled Buttons
for Renewed Garments

Some people are like extra

buttons in a crowded box

belonging to nobody

only made for back-up

waiting to be borrowed

or connected

to somebody or something . . .

Never being invited to be on a

blouse or shirt

or to

be used to hold things together

Not bound to

anybody or anything

much

or

ever touched

Some people are like little buttons

tossed in a box

forgotten but

possibly needed

for

another day

when the other one

broke up or down

or fell off

Some people are like lost and found buttons

just little usefulness

or

purpose

unidentified

But God

reassigns

reattaches

renews and sews

on buttons

where

needed

and wanted

so that

new days

are realized

for a

fresh garment to be used

for a divine transformative purpose

in the

sunlight

in spite

of the past

flight and fight

Celebration comes and

Joy   Justice

push

through

the

dirt to

bring

blossoms of

courage

and

blooms of

love

and

bouquets of hope

because faith in tomorrow was kept.

*

"This means that anyone who belongs to Christ has become a new person. The old life is gone; a new life has begun!"

1 COR 5: 17

The Refugee's Contest and Conquest

Laughter is the hallway of Escaping;

Learning is the archway of Escape;

Loving is the finish line of Flight—

Living is the trophy of Freedom.

Laughing

Laughter is like jello
        jiggling on a party day plate.
It's like cool lemonade on a hot day.
It's like warm blankets on a cold night.

Laughter is like puppies
        tumbling on their way to suck lunch.
It's like Seattle red tulips blowing in the wind.
        It's like peach azaleas appearing in southern summer sun.

Laughter is like releasing heartache
        and letting go of hate while holding hope closely.

        Laughter is like wallowing in humor

            grabbing faith

             and

            grasping trust

             while

            resting in the Lord.

A happy heart is like good medicine . . .
PROV 17:22A NCV

Recovery

Getting over an illness is like . . .
Watching a foal being born or
Witnessing a baby chick's beak punch and peck through its shell;

Emerging from radiation treatments is like . . .
Escaping from a house fire by means of a propped window ladder—
Gasping air and grabbing an arm after nearly drowning;

Pulling through surgery is like . . .
Regaining electricity after eight nights of power outage—
Drinking ice water after a bout of 98 degree Memphis Delta daze days;

Hearing a corrected diagnosis is like . . .
Spying in the city a Woodpecker or two Eurasian Collared-Doves—
Seeing a rainbow after a thunderstorm;

Lowering a medicine dosage is like . . .
Discovering a new age-defying face cream or
Sucking a fresh strawberry and mango smoothie.

". . . weeping may endure for a night but joy cometh in the morning."
Ps 30: 5b KJV

Overboard to Rescue

Too much   drinking

eating

hating

buying

talking

even loving . . .

will take you

under

and produce drowning

in the waters of life

I and IAm

tell you to

fight

face your

pain, sorrow, and plans

with friends

colleagues with

expertise in

forgiving without forgetting

Facing the fears, failures, and infractions

can help deliver you to the freedom

of a

life preserver

Do it with the

Anonymous

Organizations

Get the victory

with the Jesus

Organisms . . .

learning to love the body and fill the mind with positive

leaning toward another route of reforming old ways

Let the dependency go to the Evil One

from which it came—

Live in Now

Find a new-day hope through spirituality's path—

Face fears with new friends and faith

Escape drowning

Defuse excessive wrath

and

find dry land

while floating on a

strong steady raft

to

newness of life—

54

"Do not fear, for I have redeemed you [from captivity]; I have called you by name, you are Mine! When you pass through the waters, I will be with you. And through the rivers, they will not overwhelm you. When you walk through the fire, you will not be scorched . . . For I am the Lord your God, the Holy One of Israel, your Savior; . . ."

Isa 43: 1b-3a AMP

Turn my eyes away from worthless things; preserve my life according to your word.

Ps 119: 37 NIV

Hope Realized

To be African American in America

    is to be silent sometimes

    when you want to talk

but to speak when God directs.

To be African American in America

    means being beautiful black

                    brown

                    yellow

                    reddish and

                    rust in color

    while still

    being mostly Royal Raisin Black in tone.

To be African American in America

    shows that greatness can

    arise from tough circumstances

            and

    love can arise from hatred

            and

richness can grow through poverty's hard dirt.

To be African American in America

proves that chains and ropes

cannot erase possibilities and opportunities

when life is touched with Divinity's Hand.

To be African American in America is to

take a stand

and

take-a-knee on the football field

when the anthem is played

so that your

just and loving protest is

brought on the scene to be

plainly and honestly seen.

To be African American in the Land of Opportunity

erases some myths that were promoted

and

toted to the public—

African Americans in America

        created a string of babies who

          blasted through prejudices

          burst through

            bundles and

            burdens and

            baskets and

            bunches of

barriers that seemed unsurmountable

        but

became more tangible and tailored

    as a people pushed and pressed

    their ways toward justice and

        pass the plantations

and onto the political   religious and

commercial   athletic   artistic

theatrical   medical . . . scenes.

Being African American in America

    produced a people who

   rallied and roped the full moons

and rode into freedom

    while bleeding burdened and hunted

        but

became liberated in flights and fights

of

sanctuary and

salvation in community

unity

with the Savior's Blessings

shared and paired and spread

over hard and good times—

Being an African American is a testimonial

to Overcoming

and Outrunning

and Overturning

the topsy-turvy to

Reveal and Reverse

Madness and to then

Uncover

Dreams

of

Realized Hope.

To Alvin O. Jackson,
the Pastor of Our Pasture

With the Father's Restoring Word you have

perfumed our Oil,

lessened our toil,

scrubbed our soil,

shielded our souls from the danger of hell.

With the Son's Replenishing Word you have

prevented our mange,

widened our range,

effected our change,

nurtured our beings toward the path of safety.

With the Spirit's Refreshing Word you have

strengthened our grind,

increased our find,

nourished our minds,

watered our spirits with the draught of heaven.

*

AT THE TIME OF the few moments that it took to write this poem, Dr. Alvin O' Neal Jackson was the senior pastor of Mississippi Boulevard Christian Church (Disciples of Christ) Memphis, Tennessee. He was (and still is) a particularly gifted preacher who went on to become the pastor of National

City Christian Church(DOC) in Washington, D.C. and Park Avenue Christian Church (DOC)in New York City, NY. I will always value my friend's biblically-based, creative, colorful, passionate, and relevant preaching. This poem is a tribute to his 43 years of church shepherding, community service, and personal friendship shown to the Garrett family.

The Committed Man and
The Supernatural Parent

He was faithful to his family

even though

his family was not faithful to him

He was loyal to his children

even though

they did not care to know him

He wrote the check

poured the water

gave the things

even though

he was granted no honor or privileges

He honored his mother and father

even though

they could not and did not and would not

support his path

He had no earthly teacher

only a Divine Partner

Who demonstrated love and faith

He was a messenger of God

but

nobody gave him intended messages to

show him the way

He copied television shows

magazines

and movies

even though he had

no human patterns

The Savior sent him images

so that he could

be the shape of a Godly

man of promise

and

provision

power and prosperity

God honored God's promises

and

showed him the pat-
tern

to

be a man

who followed the

Messenger Divine

Though my father and mother forsake me, the LORD will receive me.
Teach me your way, LORD;

Ps 27:10–11A NIV

Forgiveness

Forgiveness is willing the heart's
relationship to flow in spite of . . .

Forgiveness is letting transgressions
go away from
our consciousness
so that God's love can
swell and tell the Savior's story of glorious
permission to receive pardons
for unforgiveable
and unthinkable
infractions and failures

Forgiveness is today's
walk pass grey to bright yellow
golden Son-light and
new life

Forgiveness is release of
hold-onto and
grasping dark
thoughts and black sludge

Forgiveness is golden splashes of

sun life and light

in the midst of midnights

Forgiveness is letting go of lordship

and

resisting the temptation

to reign supreme over lives

Forgiveness is choosing to forget

the hurtful offence

and to remember the fried fish, hushpuppies, iced tea . . .

friendship and peace offering

at the kitchen table

Forgiveness is fluid flowing

unstoppable respect,

love,

joy,

peace

kindness

and

acceptance

breaking into reality's consciousness and atmosphere

Forgiveness is Holy Spirit's

work and wisdom

overflowing and brimming

into the Universe.

*

When they had gone ashore, they saw a charcoal fire there, with fish on it, and bread. Jesus said to them, "Bring some of the fish that you have just caught." So Simon Peter went aboard and hauled the net ashore, full of large fish, a hundred fifty-three of them . . . Jesus said to them, "Come and have breakfast". Jesus came and took the bread and gave it to them, and did the same with the fish. This was now the third time that Jesus appeared to the disciples after he was raised from the dead.

JOHN 21: 9–11A; 12A, 13–14 NRSV

THE RISEN JESUS CHRIST forgave. So we can do the same!

The Parade Cadence

March with the footsteps of a Driving Beat;

Move to the cadence of a Living Map;

Swell with the rhythm of a Master's Touch;

Live to the winding of a Turning Key.

Do 'til the playing of a saving taps;

Share 'til the drumming of the world is o'er;

Be 'til the day The One defines your shore;

Do with your heart and do no more.

*

For in him we live, and move, and have our being . . .
ACTS 17: 28A KJV

Fred Astaire, Michael Jackson, Bruno Mars, and Prince

Light on their feet

Smiles sweet

accompanied by heaven's beat

Smooth and Sharp

and deep

Joy spreads as they dance

with precision, passion, poise

and grace

Movements reflect

the steps of God

in the

Universal dance with

people of the faith

Long legs with air being

blown on partners who

flowed and followed backward in heels

or

sideways with sticks tapping

on the tiles and pavement

with

beats of the ages reflecting the rhythm

of

Jesus' call to the

wild with understanding, mercy, and grace

God holds out his hand and loving arm

for a dance

an eternal swing

stomp and step

around the floor

before the audiences of the earth

Astaire taps, slides, and glides

as

Michael sways, twirls, and moonwalks

as

Bruno Mars marches as he leapt uptown and

steps over planets

and meets the eternal Prince of

The Purple Rain Universe

as they all continue

Dancing with the Stars!

THE MEN IN THE title of this poem are *legends* who brought and bring joy to diverse audiences through the medium of dance. The poem was written May 29, 2018 at 3am as a tribute to the gifted and creative dancers, choreographers, filmmakers, and videographers who record treasured performances so that generations of audiences can remember how God moves through the bodies and minds of committed dance artists and technologists.

Living or otherwise, these performing artists are legendary reminders that God-given talent, diligent practice, the quest for excellence, and their willingness to share gifts can bring joy to the world and glory to God. The spirituality of their movements inspires and urges us to rise above the earthly and to visit a heavenly place, if only for a moment. I and others have found that love and appreciation of the arts can be a healthy way of managing the stress of earthly challenges.

At Olivet's Altar

Remember:

    From salty raindrops

        there happens a sweet honeysuckle;

    From curdy milk

        there consequences smooth cheese;

    From hairy caterpillars

        there bursts a sleek butterfly;

    From flimsy egg yolks

        there emerges a strong eagle;

    From prickly thorns

        there rises a white rose.

Recall:

    After Spring rainstorms

        there follows an awed rainbow;

    Behind black midnights

        there tips a fresh dawn;

    Beneath dead leaflets

        there waits a live root;

Within dark kimberlite

    there hides a dear diamond;

Inside broken nutshells

    there lies the choice meat.

Believe:

    For every extended tunnel

        a passage stands there;

    For every tangled thicket

        a clearing exists there;

    For every sunburned heatwave

        a breeze floats there;

    For every blackened forest

        a meadow rests there;

    For every obscured cave

        an opening waits there.

And while they were gazing into heaven as he went, behold, two men stood by them in white robes, and said, "Men of Galilee, why do you stand looking into heaven? This Jesus, who was taken up from you into heaven, will come in the same way as you saw him go into heaven. Then they returned to Jerusalem from the mount called Olivet . . .

Acts 1: 10–12a ESV

I waited patiently for the Lord to help me,

and he turned to me and heard my cry.

He lifted me out of the pit of despair, out of the mud and the mire.

He set my feet on solid ground and steadied me as I walked along.

He has given me a new song to sing, a hymn of praise to our God.

Ps 40: 1–3 NLT

The Sanity, Sanctuary, Solidarity, Solace, and Smiles of Friendships

Carolyn the Resourceful Motivating Mentor

Clarke the Laughter

Nettie the Beauty Giver

Lois the Listener

Jean the Bells

John the Legs

Solomon the Rocks

Charlie David the Reminder

Millie the Prayer

Ronald the Artist Messenger

Celeste the Forever Neighbor

Beverly the Sister Cousin

Sylvia the Earnest Christ Seeker

Ursula the Healer

Wesley the Watchtower

Thank you, O Sweet Holy Spirit God, for my sacred circle of gifted friends.

THIS VERSE IS DEDICATED with thanks to Carolyn N. Tisdale, Nettie V. Tipton, Lois D. Madison, Jean E. Johnson, John Baker, Solomon M. Garrett Jr., Millie Anderson, Ronald Lane, Celeste Turner, Beverly B. Cox, Sylvia

Albritton, Ursula W. Elliot, Allen Wesley, 5-year-old granddaughter Clarke Mackie, and 10-year-old grandson Charlie D. Mackie.

Soon afterward, Jesus began going around from one city and village to another, preaching and proclaiming the good news of the kingdom of God. The twelve [disciples] were with Him, and also some women who had been healed of evil spirits and diseases: Mary, called Magdalene [from the city of Magdala in Galilee], from whom seven demons had come out, and Joanna, the wife of Chuza, Herod's household steward, and Susanna, and many others who were contributing to their support out of their private means [as was the custom for a rabbi's disciples].

LUKE 8: 1–3 AMP

To the Queen Ant, Lady Leah

Oh how tragic to bare and bear for

    all your living without love

Oh how tearing to think and note

    all your being and feel no love

Oh how troubling to bare and bore for

    all your giving within love

Oh how torrid to thirst and beg for

    all your tastes and not love

Oh how thwarting to spray and sprout for

    all your planting and find no love

Oh how tricking to pick and plot

    for all of your choosing and be unloved

Oh how tested to temper and tip for

    all your mapping and see no love . . .

Oh how tortured to bare and wish for

      all your dying without love

Oh how turbid to twist and twirl

      for all your slumbering and feel no love

Oh how trusting to tote and topple for

      all your grasping within love

Oh how sordid to sail and scale for

      all your flying and not love

Oh how cursed to kiss and kneel for

      all your curtsies and find no love

Oh how brazen to model and mask for

      all your carbons and be unloved

Oh how horrid to hope and hop

      for all your hosting and no love . . .

Oh how testing to bear and boast for

all your babies without love

Oh how cheated to slave and serve for

all your coupling and feel no love

Oh how touching to tramp and trump for

all your trusting within love

Oh how willing to whip and wail for

all your days and not love

Oh how lonely to look and lose for

all your praying and find no love

Oh how ignored to rant and rave

for all of your utterance and be unloved

Oh how poisoned to paint and primp

for all of your grooming and get no love . . .

Oh how taxing to bear and know for

all your mating without love

Oh how wretched to weep and wrench for

all your gifts and feel no love

Oh how moving to sit and slip for

all your shaping within love

Oh how damning to delve and do

for all of your driving and not love

Oh now chilling to chide and cringe for

all your pleas and find no love

Oh how draining to drip and dip

for all of your dreaming and be unloved

Oh how tiring to trust and thrust for

all your caressing without lust . . .

Oh now moving to scrape and scrap for

all your climbing without love

Oh how limpid to linger and long for

all your smiles and feel no love

Oh how hopeless to hem and helm

for all of your hoisting within love

Oh how hapless to have and hold

for all of your union and not love

O how crushing to clasp and croon

for all of your calling and find no love

Oh how fallow to fail and fall for

all your eggs and be unloved

Oh how bruising to burst and bust

for all of your fission with no love . . .

Oh how shaming to share and shadow

for all your mating without love

Oh how murdered to migrate and mix for

all your lusts and feel no love

Oh how stripping to strain and stretch

for all of your struggling and find no love

Oh how hollow to hold and hope

for all of your joining and not love

Oh how aching to ask and answer for

all your quizzing and find no love

Oh how baffling to love and labor

for all of your tenure and know no love

Oh how human to want and wish

for all of your mating only to yield love*

Oh how wondrous to weld and win for

all your pairing and know self-love

Oh how grateful to grasp and see for

all your gazing and feel some love

Oh how soothing to sail and soar for

all your growing in real love

Oh how gracious to give and get from

all your friends and find much love

Oh how winning to wean and wander from

all your scraping and see True Love

Oh how honored to hold and hope

for all of your rebirth and be so loved

Oh how royal to rest and reign

for all of your sleeping with The Love.

As it was with the devalued, unappreciated, unattractive first wife of Jacob called Leah, so it is with many women. Her story is found in Genesis 29, 31, and 35. In this tense, unfulfilling relationship where Leah initially focused primarily on *her man,* she found *at last,* praise for God who loved her unconditionally. (Gen: 29: 35) Later in life it seems that Jacob, curiously, had some change of heart because he directed that his remains after death be placed in the family gravesite where he laid to rest his parents (Isaac and Rebecca), grandparents (Abraham and Sarah), and Leah. (Gen 49:29–33)

To the Seashell, Helen

There the shell lay;

        in rich color clothed,

        in perfect shape formed,

Enough beauty at first glance

To put one in a trance.

There it lay prized ajar on my palm;

        bathed by the sea's scent,

        marked by the ocean's sound,

        filled with an unexpected

            substance,

A closer look reveals meat

The likes of which is sweet.

There my open hinged treasure lay;

        with singular softness gifted,

        with a refined gem blessed,

        by the sea's ancient knowledge

            touched.

I thank the Sculptor of this piece

For allowing its release.

*

As a young woman, I was a member of Olivet Baptist Church in Memphis, Tennessee where my pastor's wife named Helen was one of the most beautiful women I had ever met. I admired her since she served as a parent, wife, sincere Christian, a paid professional leader, and a personal confidante who exhibited candor, intelligence, and wisdom. I wrote this tribute to her in the 1980's. After this poem was written, she served for several years on the Membership Committee of the Jackson County, MO Links, Incorporated. Even now at the publishing of this poem, Ms Helen Whalum Rogers, since 2009, continues to serve as one of the first female deacons of Metropolitan Missionary Baptist Church in Kansas City, Missouri.

To David, the Archer's Bow

This sleek and slender stick
Races to its mark.
This straight and keen shaft
Searches for tree bark.

This stem of wood and feather
is the reaper of all glory.
This strip of branch—a twig
is the star of each story.

Whether the Eye be

colored circles or game,

matted straw or doe not tame,

It is the little stick

Who gets credit for the hit.

But . . .

The strong and smooth board
Guides the little spears.
The curved and flexible timber
Effects the target's pierce.

The device of cord and lumber

is the support of each attack.

The thing of rope and fiber

keeps small marksmen on their track.

Whether the Eye be

livened hopes or crushed fears

realized visions or training of peers

It is on the Archer with sturdy bow

My praises I do bestow.

THE LATE MINISTER DAVID N. Flagg was a high school mathematics teacher, a church choir director, the visionary founder of Memphis Community Singers, Inc., and a gifted musician who trained and mentored teenagers, young adults, and his peers for over 30 years. This poem written in his memory is dedicated to all teachers and leaders who dare to prayerfully mentor, train, and touch others . . . especially young people.

To the Gift, Jean

A new friend is like

>an oasis springing from a desert;

>a single yellow rose rising from thorns;

>a new green shoot popping from the crusty earth;

>an embryo progressing to birth.

A new found friend is like

>a single star revealed on a cloudy night;

>a pearl released from a sea of shells;

>a reformed caterpillar bursting to its butterfly life;

>Peace finding a sinner amid earth's strife.

A new friend is

>a packet from the Magi;

>sustenance for a thirsty heart;

>worthy of my listening and planning;

>deserving of my freely given understanding.

A new friend is you.

Leader and People in Formation

To J. Lawrence who is learning to lead and love

a people-of-faith

who

are called to be greater than before—

To J. L. Turner, the turner of hearts

who is destined to lead the community

into a place of greater

justice and

more social responsibility and unity—

To the young man preacher-teacher

whose eyes are focused on righteousness, revival, and reform

in the face of a trumped-up,

tumultuous,

topsy-turvy,

turning,

tumbling

world—

To the pastor

who is gathering sheep

for the pasture that has expanded from those only eating
and sharing hay

into those who are consuming cyberspace grass
while

still serving people of the taste-and-see God of the Ages
and Fresh Generations.

*Oh taste and see that the Lord is good! Blessed is the man who takes
refuge in him!*

Ps34: 8 ESV

THIS POEM IS DEDICATED to Rev. Dr. Jason Lawrence Turner, the senior
pastor of Mississippi Boulevard Christian Church (Disciples of Christ)—
the author's present church community located in Memphis, Tennessee.

Valentine to My Sweet Heart

Love is

    an ice cube on a parched day

    a yellow rose blooming in hard brittle clay

    the smell of crisp bacon after a night's sleep

    the softness of a hand on a cheek

    a single smile in a room of frowns

    a kiss on the back with no others around;

Love is

    a light touch of the fingertips to my lips

    the scent of hair that has been perfume dipped

    a cup of steaming hot chocolate surrounded by snow

    a floating white swan amid a flock of crows;

Love is

    an oasis in the hot desert

    an igloo in the cold Artic

    a campfire on the lonely prairie

    a lighthouse on the dark sea;

Love can be

      a gasp for air as passions spin

      a clump of gold at the rainbow's end

      a sliver of silver in a cloud's gloom;

Love is

      a prayer whispered in earnest with an answer floating swiftly on the wind

      the new me surrounded by and filled with the new you.

Place me like a seal over your heart, like a seal on your arm.
For love is as strong as death, its passion as enduring as the grave.
SONG OF SONGS 8: 6A NLT

The Bride

A yellow rosebud and honeysuckle

A bouquet of Baby's Breath and lace

A love song and sacred scriptures

Words of Promise spoken with friends

A last dance and a first one

An expected season of fruitfulness

and on-going laughter while nesting

A hand held with hopefulness

and faith in future blessings

Connection and Joy clothed in Love

*

Pat's Wedding-Day Smile

If you see my face blush today,
  it is because my mind is pleased—
Pleased with a man who is strong enough
    to pour out his earnest love
    yet sure enough to spur mine on.

If you see my eyes mist today,
  it is because my heart is filled—
Filled with a man who is wise enough
    to blot out his foolish anger
    and kind enough to calm mine
    down;
Filled with a man who is brave enough
    to test out his newest idea
    and sweet enough to think mine
    through.

If you see my mouth smile today,
  it is because my life is blessed—
Blessed with a man who is frank enough
    to let out his inmost need
    yet free enough to hear mind out;
Blessed with a God who is keen enough
    to point out our freshest course
    and good enough to lift us up.

My poem first appeared in *Womenpsalms,* which was published in 1992 by Saint Mary's Press.

An Empowered Sister
in a New SUV is Like . . .

A Queen Bee whose hive has been destroyed . . .

A Mother whose son has been deployed . . .

A Woman whose man is unemployed . . .

A Nursing Mother whose breasts are engorged . . .

A Working Mom whose grievances have been ignored . . .

A Loving Wife who has been trumped by a whore . . .

A Manic Driving Witch who is defeating road rage . . .

A Betrayed Lover who is overcoming the fray . . .

A Freed Female who has risen above payday . . .

A Soaring Eagle released from a cage . . .

A Spirit-filled Recovering Woman no longer enraged . . .

A Freed Girlfriend in a fresh life stage . . .

I waited patiently for the Lord. He turned to me and heard my cry. He lifted me out of the pit of destruction, out of the sticky mud. He stood me on a rock and made my feet steady. He put a new song in my mouth, a song of praise to our God. Many people will see this and worship him. Then they will trust the Lord.

Ps 40:1–3 NCV

God's Gifts

Daughters are like angels
    falling
        from
            my
            Fallopian tubes
     and
bouncing onto an earth
  that is moving slowly
          and
          steadily
     in the
      midst of change
        and
         transition.
  They land in my arms
    but
are the property
    possession-gifts of God the Creator
    to
a waiting world.

        Amen. . . So be it . . . So it is

DEDICATED WITH LOVE TO *Dana D. Garrett, Marloe D. G., Clarke, and Cooper Mackie—*

Finding and Experiencing
Jesus is Like . . .

Seeing a double rainbow

and

a swan float.

Touching clean hair

and

a cotton ball.

Hearing kittens purr

and

a mother's hum.

Witnessing a Lightning Bolt

strike, splinter, split, and re-shape an old oak tree.

Watching a grandchild's birth

and

snow fall.

Smelling Hawaiian blue water

and

bacon cooking.

Biting a juicy orange

and

sweet watermelon.

*If anyone belongs to Christ, there is a new creation. The old things have
gone; everything is made new!*

2 Cor 5:17 NCV

From Obscure Darkness to Joy

The August 2017 solar eclipse had to be experienced

before the layer of night ended

suddenly to show the sun again.

The moon covered the sun

but then

the sunshine burst through

to the covered-shaded eyes of

people who applauded

the Overcoming Victory—

The sun survived

as also did your spiritual light.

After the eerie shadowed dimness left,

Bright-Joy newness of life came . . .

Tell this news with shouts of joy to the people;

spread it everywhere on earth.

Is 48:20 NCV

THE YEAR 2017 WAS a time of extreme world-wide—sometimes life-threatening—weather conditions and bizarre polarizing political positions. And after each phenomenon occurred, some people panicked, the earth continued, the sunlight returned, and the brilliant Light of the Savior prevailed in the lives of people-of-faith who prayed and believed.

The Creator's Ultimate
Truth and Beauty

For every star in the sky
there is a reason to be grateful—

For every color in the rainbow
there is a promise to see dreams come to reality—

For every moment that the moon shines
there is a hope for a dawning to come to fruition.

The heavens are telling the glory of God . . .
Ps 19:1A NRSV

God continued,
"This is the sign of the covenant I am making between me and you and
everything living around you and everyone living after you. I'm putting
my rainbow in the clouds, a sign of the covenant between me and the
Earth."
Gen 9: 12–13 MSG

God's Yellow Rose

Whether the weather is

    extreme cold or hot

        or the plot of ground is soggy or hard—

I am the yellow rose who

    catches the sequined sparkle

    and reflects it in the dewy

            morning

              droplets.

I am sparkle in the midst of thorns.

I am the nestled and sprinkled yellow rose that

brings out the bride's bouquet with touches of

            love and joy

            promised.

I am the stubborn   strong   sturdy

    clinging   climbing vine that winds

    my way up the side of an eight foot

        fence or wall and stretches

        my beauty

toward the sky

where Jesus

    the Spirit of the Lord God

    kisses my petals

        for infinite eternity . . .

I am God's yellow rose who sees

    honest red, black, blue, and green

    but

    helps others to overcome and re-color their adversities with

        The Wonderful Counselor's Bright Light.

I am the chosen yellow rose who splashes Son-shine and clear cheer on the subject

    so that willing people are high-lighted

    lifted and gifted

    with Spirituality and A Fresh Path to God's Love . . .

Amen So be it and So it is

The New Beginning

You are the star on which the Cord of Life is suspending glorious ways
for the worlds to see.

About the Author

Cozette Rogers Garrett is an ordained Christian Church (Disciples of Christ) minister who has served God and God's people for over 30 years in both lay and clergy—paid and volunteer—positions. She teaches, preaches, and trains, in a variety of settings.

She received an earned Doctor of Ministry from United Theological Seminary at Dayton, Ohio where her main focus was Faith and Health in Community and Congregations. With heavy interest in Pastoral Care, Dr. Cozette graduated with honors from Memphis Theological Seminary where she received her Master of Divinity. Her days studying at University of Memphis resulted in a Bachelor of Arts in Journalism and Speech & Drama Education. Her sorority sisters from Delta Sigma Theta Sorority, Inc. helped her to become the first African American to be elected to the University's Student Government.

Rev. Garrett served in many church and community positions including a local church pastor, associate pastor, program director, hospital and hospice chaplain, public assistance eligibility trainer, and adjunct seminary professor. At her present home church, which is Mississippi Boulevard Christian Church (DOC) in Memphis, she facilitates a weekly life group and often conducts premarital sessions for new couples.

The title of her first published book is *Diamond Discoveries of a Woman Preacher: A Word for Female Clergy and Those Wanting to Understand Them*.

Dr." Coz" is the mother of two adult daughters—Dana and Marloe. Charlie Mackie and Marloe G. Mackie are the parents of her three grandchildren—Charlie David, Clarke, and Cooper. For over 40 years she has lived in Memphis, TN with her husband, Solomon M. Garrett.